Cooking

Ruth Thomson

Franklin Watts
London • New York • Sydney • Toronto

Note for parents and teachers

The Changing Times series is soundly based on the requirements of the new History Curriculum. Using the device of four generations of a real family, the author combines reminiscences of this family with other people's oral evidence. The oral history is matched with photographs and other contemporary sources. Many other lessons are hidden in the text, which practises the skills of chronological sequencing, gives reference to a timeline and introduces the language and vocabulary of the past. Young children will find much useful information here, as well as a new understanding of the recent history of everyday situations and familiar things.

© 1992 Franklin Watts

Franklin Watts
96 Leonard Street
London
EC2A 4RH

Franklin Watts Australia
14 Mars Road
Lane Cove
NSW 2066

UK ISBN: 0 7496 0891 9

Editor: Sarah Ridley
Designer: Michael Leaman
Educational consultant: John West
Photographer: Peter Millard

Acknowledgements: The publishers would like to thank the following people and organisations for their help with the preparation of this book: Lisa Chaney; Jessie Baker, Jessie Ridley and Suzanne Ridley; Kim Sinclair of Kitchen and Country Antiques and Diana Green for the loan of items from their collections.

A CIP catalogue record for this book is available, from the British Library.

Printed in Malaysia

Contents

This is our kitchen.

We cook most food on the hob
and bake cakes and pies
in the electric oven.

Dirty dishes are washed
in the dishwasher.

We keep milk, butter, eggs
and other foods that need
to keep cool in the fridge,
and frozen foods in the freezer.

Sometimes Mum uses
the microwave to cook
quick meals.

We make toast in the toaster for breakfast.

We boil water in the jug kettle for tea and coffee.

We use a food processor for mixing pastry and cakes and shredding vegetables.

These are some of our cooking utensils.

Bread knife

Egg whisk

Grater

Sieve

Spatula

Kitchen knife

Slice

Ice-cream scoop

Tin opener

Measuring jug

Rolling pin

Wooden spoons

Lemon squeezer

Corkscrew

7

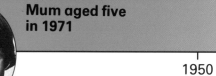
I asked Mum what her kitchen was like when she was young.

She said,

'We cooked on a gas stove. It had a plate rack and a grill pan.'

'The kettle was heated on the stove. It whistled when the water boiled.'

'A geyser heated the water.
The gas made
a loud popping noise
when it came on.'

'Milk, eggs and meat
were kept cool
in a meat safe.'

When Mum's family moved house,
they had a new kitchen with fitted units.

Mum said,

'There was such excitement when we got a fridge.
It was taller than I was.'

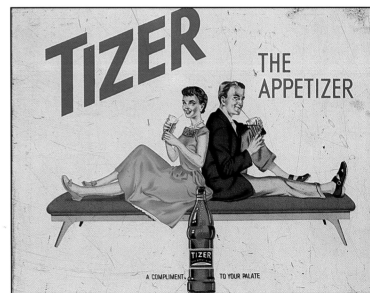

'For breakfast, we ate
cereals and toast.
On Sundays, there was
cooked breakfast.
I liked beans on toast.'

'My favourite drinks were
Tizer, Peardrax and lemonade.'

I asked Granny about the kitchen
her family had when she was young.

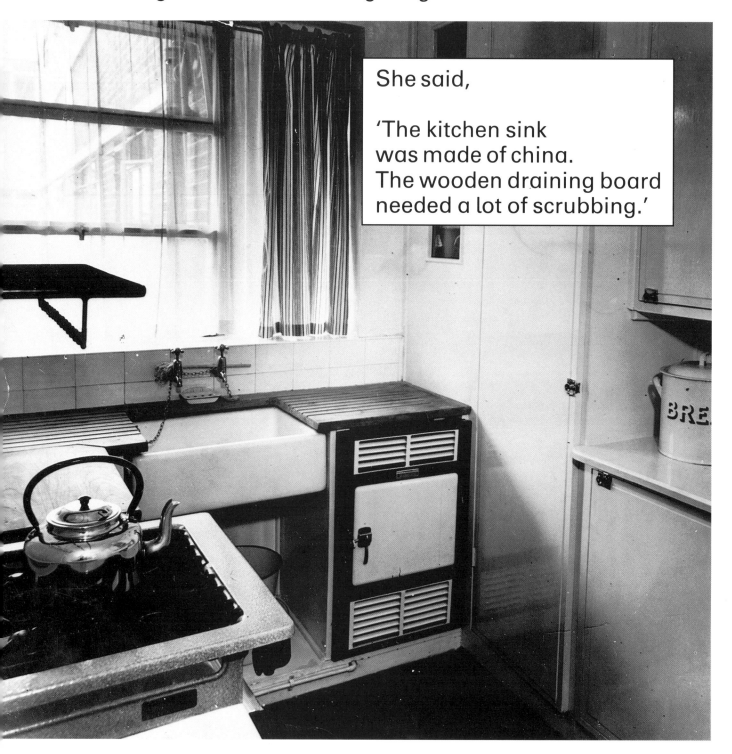

She said,

'The kitchen sink
was made of china.
The wooden draining board
needed a lot of scrubbing.'

'We had a gas cooker on legs. It had a grill for making toast.'

'We didn't have a fridge. Food was kept cold in the larder. It had red floor tiles.'

'Some families had a fridge. They were quite expensive.'

Granny said,

'We ate bread and jam for breakfast,
stews or sausages for lunch
and sandwiches or toast at teatime.'

1930s toaster

Who spotted
SPOTTED DICK?

Mc Dougall's
the SELF-RAISING FLOUR that never varies

'My favourite
dishes were
puddings.'

14

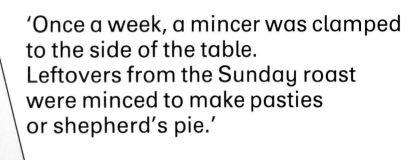

'Once a week, a mincer was clamped to the side of the table.
Leftovers from the Sunday roast were minced to make pasties
or shepherd's pie.'

'Some of our neighbours used a kitchen range
to cook on.
Others had Agas
or electric ovens.'

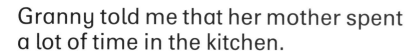
Granny told me that her mother spent a lot of time in the kitchen.

She said,

'My mother made all her own scones, and teacakes for teatime.'

'My aunt made her own mincemeat at Christmastime.'

'In January, she made
enough marmalade
to last us the rest of the year.'

'In summertime,
she made jams and jellies
with gooseberries, redcurrants
and cherries.'

When the Second World War came, some foods became very scarce.

Granny said,

'Everyone had a ration book to take shopping with them.'

'You could only buy small amounts of butter, cheese and meat each, so there was enough for all.'

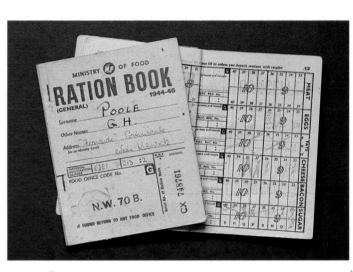

'The government issued cookery leaflets to show people how to make best use of their food.'

'I remember we used dried egg from a packet and dried milk from a tin. The taste was all right once you got used to it.'

'Sometimes our friends ate at a wartime kitchen, especially if their parents were busy with war work.'

Great-granny told me there was no electricity
at all in her house when she was young.
There wasn't a fridge or an electric cooker.

She said,

'Food was cooked on a coal-fired range.
Saucepans were put on top.
Pies were cooked in the oven.
Rubbish was burned in the fire.'

'A cast-iron kettle was kept hot on top of the stove all day long.'

'Bread was toasted on a toasting fork in front of the fire.'

'Knives used to rust, because they were made of steel. We didn't have stainless steel then. One of my jobs was to clean and polish them on a knifeboard.'

I asked Great-granny
where food was kept.

She said,

'Fresh food
was kept in the larder.
It had a stone floor
and a marble shelf to
help keep things cool.'

'Bread was kept
in an enormous
earthenware crock.
The bread board
was its lid.'

'The milk jug stood in a bowl of cold water to stop the milk from going off.
A muslin cloth on top kept flies out.'

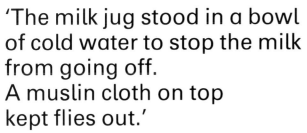

'Meat was kept under a gauze meat cover so flies and mice couldn't get at it.'

'Cheese was kept in a covered cheese dish or in a cheese cloth in the larder.'

23

Great-granny said,

'We had the same meals every day of every week.'

'Roast on a Sunday.
Cold leftovers on a Monday,
which was busy washday.
Meat pie on a Tuesday.
Meat stew on Wednesday.
Meat pudding on Thursday.
Sausages on Friday.
Saturday was whatever
Mother felt like —
rabbit was a favourite.'

'At bedtime, we drank cocoa and ate toast and dripping.'

'Friday was baking day.
My mother baked cakes, biscuits and pies.
The house smelt warm and welcoming.'

These are some of the kitchen utensils that Great-granny had when she was young. They are all made of metal, wood or pottery.

Potato masher

Mortar and pestle (for grinding up spices)

Colander

Sugar nippers

Pudding mould

Knives

Pattypan

Can opener

Corkscrew

Vegetable chopper

Spoon

Biscuit cutters

Which ones have you never seen before?
Compare these utensils with those on page 7.
Have any of them changed shape or material?

Grater

Storage jar

Coffee
grinder

Gravy
strainer

Spice
box

Jelly mould

Nutmeg
grater

Whisks

Things to do

Which of these objects
do you have in your kitchen?
Which ones do you think your parents,
grandparents or great-grandparents had?
Look back through the book to help you.

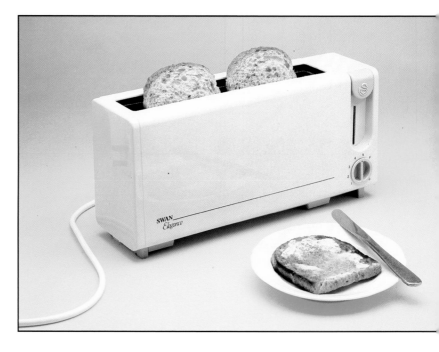

Do you ever have take-away meals?

Ask some grown-ups what take-away meals
they had when they were young.

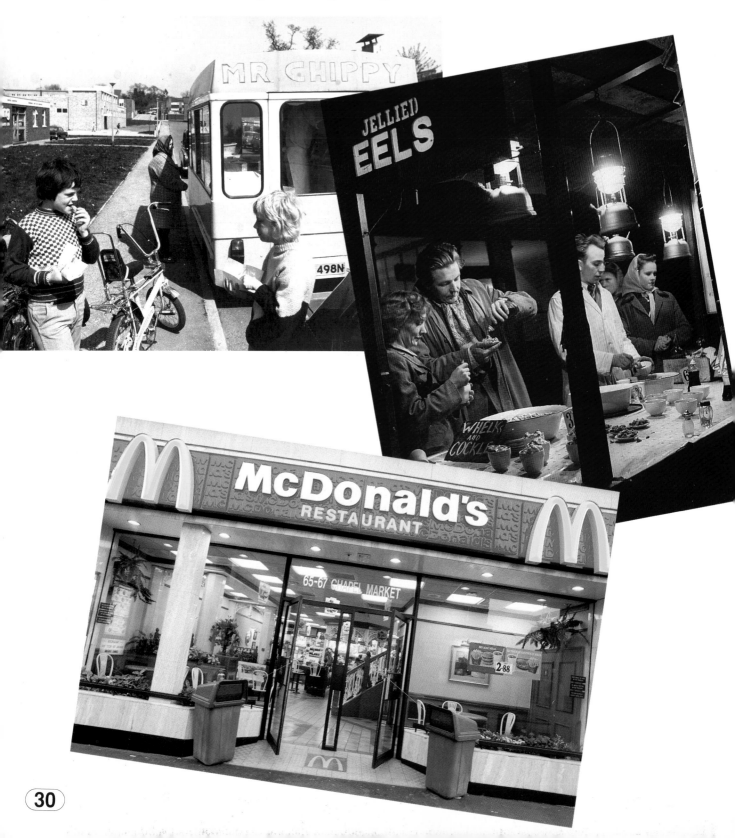

This is what Great-granny's kitchen was like. What is the same about it as your kitchen? What is different?

Index

Photographs: Advertising Archives 10, 11(tl), 11(tr); Barnaby's cover (bl), 8(b), 13(tr), 17(t); Beamish title page (t), 23(t), 23(c); © British Gas plc endpapers, 8(t); Cadbury Ltd 24(b); Lisa Chaney 22(tr), 31; © Coggs Manor Farm Museum cover (tl), 20; Mary Evans Picture Library 14(br); Chris Fairclough 4(br), 5(bl), 6(b); Sally and Richard Greenhill 4(l); Hulton Picture Company cover (tr), 12, 14(t), 24(t), 30(tr); with thanks to the Trustees of the Imperial War Museum 19(b); Magnet plc cover (br), title page (b), 4-5(t); thanks to McDonald's 30(b); Peter Millard imprint page, 6(tl), 6(tr), 7, 9(b), 14(bl), 15(t), 21(all), 22(b), 23(b), 25, 26-27, 28, 29(c), 29(bl), 29(br); Moulinex Swan Holdings 29(t); Museum of East Anglian Life 18(bl), 18(br); Robert Opie 11(b), 13(br), 16(t), 18(t), 19(t); Topham Picture Source 15(b), 16(b), 30(tl); thanks to Zanussi Ltd 5(tr), 13(l).